Mighty Machines
BIKES

Graham

QED Publishing

First published in the UK in 2008 by
QED Publishing
A Quarto Group company
226 City Road
London EC1V 2TT

www.qed-publishing.co.uk

A catalogue record for this book is available from the British Library.

Printed and bound in China

ISBN 978 1 84835 033 5

Author Ian Graham
Designed by Phil and Traci Morash (Fineline Studios)
Editor Paul Manning
Picture Researcher Claudia Tate

Publisher Steve Evans
Creative Director Zeta Davies

Picture credits
(t = top, b = bottom, c = centre, l = left, r = right, FC = front cover)
Alamy Eric Nathan 14, Steve Hamblin 15
Corbis Leo Mason 7, Marvy! 10, Richard H Cohen 18, Tim de Waele 19,
Anthony West 22 bc
Ridgeback 4
Shutterstock Digitalsport-photoagency FC, Marcel Jancovic 1,
Cornel Achirei 5, Tom Richards 8, Keith Robinson 9, Maxim Petrichuk 11,
Ravshan Mirzaitov 12, Lucian Coman 13, Maxim Petrichuk 16,
Max Blain 17, Timothy Large 20, 21, Anthony Hall, 22br

Words in **bold** can be found
in the glossary on page 23.

Contents

What is a **bike?**

Bikes are a useful way to travel around. Most bikes have two wheels that move when the rider pushes down on the pedals. A motorbike has an engine. It can go much faster than a pedal bike.

Pushing the pedals turns the back wheel and makes the bike move. Squeezing the brake handles makes the bike stop.

brake handles

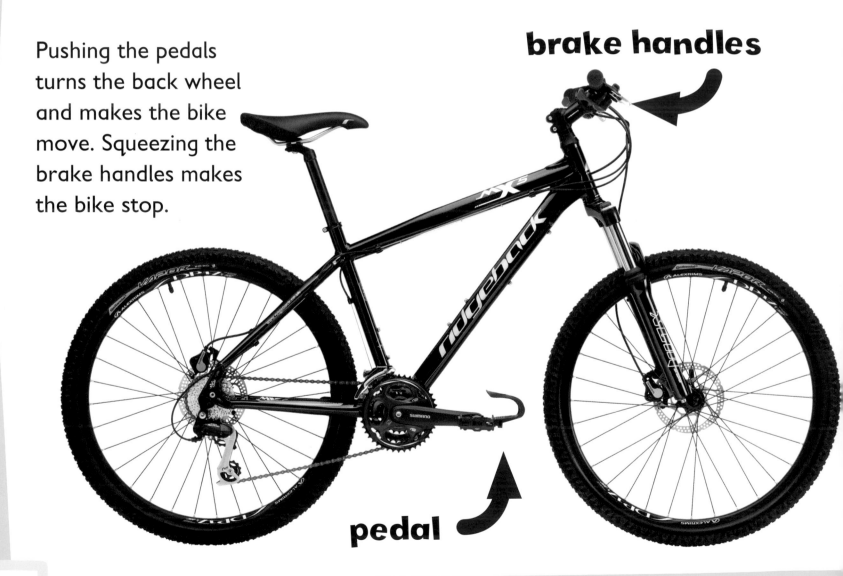

pedal

There are all sorts of different motorbikes. Sports bikes and racing bikes are fast. **Trail** bikes are for riding off-road, on dirt tracks.

A motorbike's engine sits under the seat in the middle of a strong frame called the chassis. A chain linked to the engine drives the back wheel.

Superbikes

A superbike is a light sports motorbike with an incredibly powerful engine to give it extra zip. Superbikes are among the fastest bikes on the road.

Motorcycle racing is a really popular sport. Motorbike races can be held on road tracks, special racing circuits or off-road.

To go round corners at speed, superbike riders lean over until they almost touch the ground.

Motocross

Motocross races are held on hilly dirt tracks full of **obstacles** and jumps. The bikes have knobbly **tyres** to grip the track.

Riders must think fast to work out the quickest way round the track. They need to be fit to take part, so they train hard.

Motocross riders jump high into the air on their bike. They can be injured if they are thrown off the bike at high speed.

Motocross bikes need good **suspension** and springy wheels to cushion them against bumps and jolts.

Easy riders

Harley-Davidsons are big, powerful motorbikes with lots of shiny **chrome**. They are heavy bikes, made for sitting back and cruising along the open road.

Some owners **customize** their bikes by adding extra chrome fittings and high handlebars. These bikes are sometimes called choppers, because their owners chop off the parts they do not need.

The Harley-Davidson's **exhaust** is famous for the deep, throaty roar it makes!

exhaust

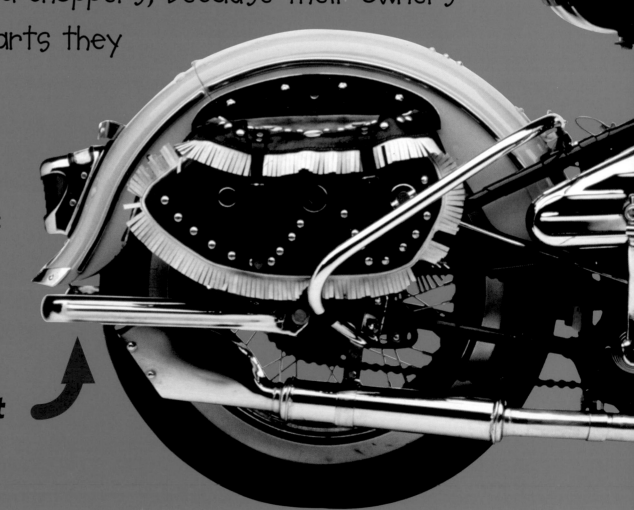

Many US police forces use Harley-Davidson motorbikes because they are fast, yet also good for weaving in and out of **traffic**.

11

Quad bikes

A quad bike is a motorbike with four wide wheels. It is useful for moving across soft or muddy ground without getting stuck. Many farmers use quad bikes to get around their land.

At quad sports events, riders race their bikes over all kinds of ground, from snow and ice to beaches and sandy desert.

This farmer is using a quad bike to help round up a flock of sheep.

Most quad bikes have four-wheel drive. The engine drives all four wheels. This helps the wheels to keep a grip on rough or bumpy ground.

13

Scooters

For zipping through busy city traffic, nothing beats a scooter. It has a smaller engine and wheels than other types of motorbikes. Instead of sitting astride the bike, riders place their feet on a footrest between the wheels.

A motorscooter taxi whisks passengers through the busy streets of Bangkok, Thailand.

A scooter is not as fast as a motorbike, but it is good for short journeys around town.

In Italy, a scooter is the favourite way of getting around.

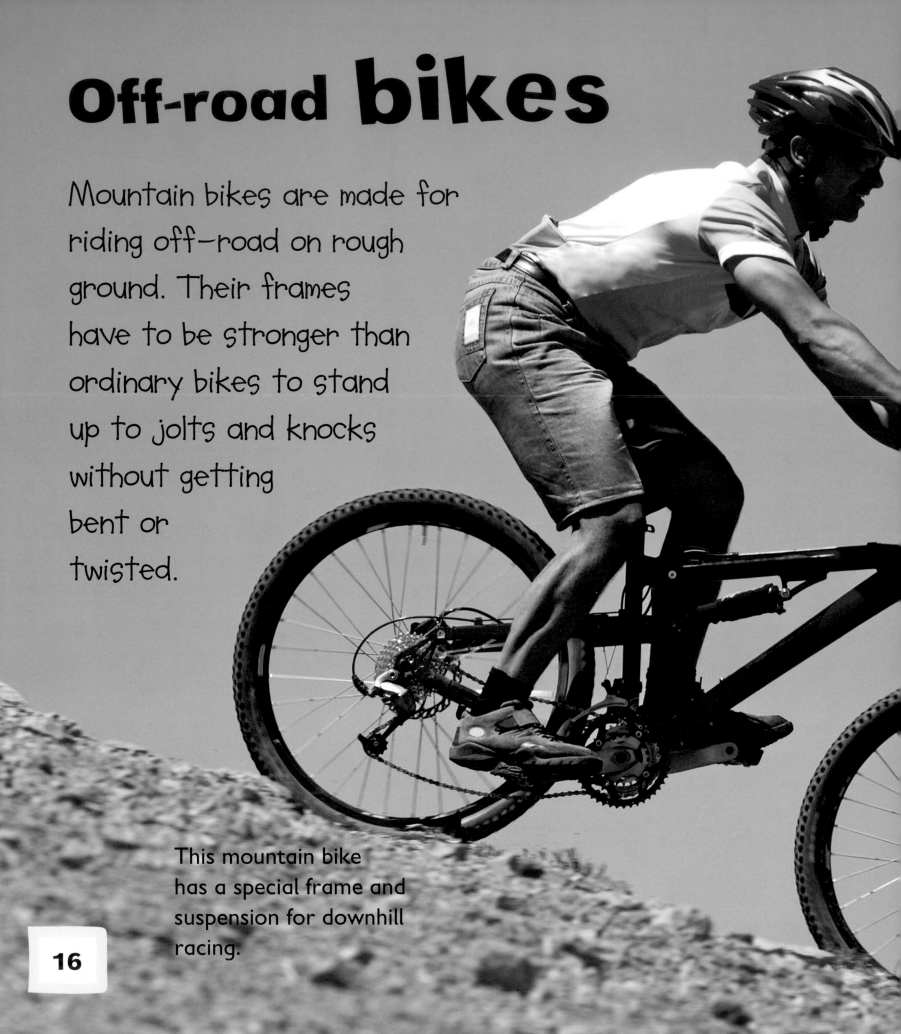

Off-road bikes

Mountain bikes are made for riding off-road on rough ground. Their frames have to be stronger than ordinary bikes to stand up to jolts and knocks without getting bent or twisted.

This mountain bike has a special frame and suspension for downhill racing.

A mountain bike can cope with rough forest trails where no ordinary bike can go.

Mountain bikes have fat, knobbly tyres and lots of **gears** to make it easier to go up steep hills.

Racing bikes

Racing bikes are built for speed. Their tyres are so thin, they hardly touch the ground.

Some racing bikes are made especially for long races along roads. Others, called track bikes, are used for indoor races in **velodromes**.

Handcycles are powered by the rider's hands instead of their feet. These racing bikes are popular with disabled riders.

Track bikes often have solid wheels that slip through the air faster than normal wheels with **spokes**.

BMX bikes

BMX stands for Bicycle Motocross. Riders tear round a circuit of bumps and jumps on a small-wheeled bike with a single gear. BMX bikes are made for racing on hilly dirt tracks and for freestyle stunt riding.

With their small frames, fat wheels and high handlebars, BMX bikes are great for doing tricks, such as wheelies and jumps.

BMX riders need to wear helmets and full protective gear in case of pile-ups.

21

Activities

- Which picture shows a bike's saddle, handlebars and a gear wheel?

- Make a drawing of your favourite bike. What sort of bike is it? Does it have big wheels or small wheels? What colour is it?

- Write a story about the bike ride you would most like to go on. It could be anywhere in the world – or even on another planet! Where would you like to go? Who would you like to meet? What do you think you might see? How long would it take?

- Which of these bikes would a racing cyclist ride?

Glossary

Chrome
A shiny coating on metal.

Customize
To alter or add to something to make it special for the owner.

Exhaust
A pipe that carries waste gases away from the engine of a bike.

Gear
A toothed wheel that lets the pedals turn the wheels of a bike at different speeds.

Obstacle
Something that is placed in the way of a bike to slow it down.

Spokes
Thin, metal wires that connect the centre of a bicycle wheel with the outer edge.

Suspension
A set of springs that connects a bike's wheels and frame to give a smoother ride. The springs let the wheels follow bumps in the ground, while the rest of the bike moves along smoothly.

Traffic
Cars, trucks, buses and other vehicles that use the roads.

Trail
A dirt track for riding motorbikes off-road.

Tyre
A rubber tube filled with air that fits around the edge of a wheel.

Velodrome
A race track specially designed for bike racing.

Index